SEO for WordPress:

How To Get Your Website on Page #1 of Google...Fast!

[2nd Edition]

By

Kent Mauresmo
Anastasiya Petrova

Copyright

Contents

Introduction

"Do You Want To Discover How Easily Rank Higher On Google?"

In this updated book, we're going show you how to easily blast past your competition in the search engine results. Many SEO companies will charge you $500-$1000 just to analyze your website which is truly a rip-off.

My name is Kent Mauresmo and I'm one of the bloggers at www.read2learn.net. I'm also one the authors of the kindle eBook, **"How to Build a Website with WordPress...Fast!"** If you've already read that eBook, then you should be familiar with a few of our basic SEO techniques.

In this updated book, we'll show you exactly how to fully optimize your WordPress website/blog to increase your chances of showing up on the first page of Google. After your website is fully optimized, we'll show you where to go to analyze your entire website for FREE to make sure it's perfect!

After you tweak your websites settings, we'll next show you exactly how to get backlinks to your website to boost your rankings on Google fast! We'll also show you how to manually build backlinks, and the automated way if you're super lazy.

Depending on your niche, I can't guarantee that you'll end up on the first page of Google overnight or EVER! Some people try to rank on the first page of Google for almost impossible keyword phrases like, "*Used Cars*" so your results may vary.

I guarantee you that after you read this book, you'll **never** consider hiring an SEO company again. SEO is not as hard as most people think. It's actually just common sense, and once you know the secrets, <u>it's easy</u>.

The techniques you'll discover will <u>boost your</u> websites rankings fast. Depending on how competitive your niche is, I feel confident in saying that 90% of your <u>competition will virtually disappear</u> once you apply what you learn today.

<u>DISCLAIMER</u>: This book will have some flaws and maybe a few grammatical errors. If you read for style, or for literary quality, then this probably isn't the book for you. The only objective of this book is to show you how too easily:

1. Do your own S.E.O. for WordPress
2. Dominate 90% of your competition
3. Get on the 1st page of Google

<u>What are some of the updates in this book?</u>

Some of the updates in this book include showing you how to:

1. Use Google's new Keyword Planner Tool
2. Use the updated version of Traffic Travis to improve your on page S.E.O.

If you're ready, then let's get started!

Chapter 1.

Advance Keyword Research

Since Google is the most popular search engine in the world, we will use their Keyword Planner Tool. Go to http://adwords.google.com/keywordplanner and make sure that you're signed into your Gmail account first.

You're going to arrive at a screen that'll ask you "What would you like to do?" Click on the column that says "Search for new keyword and ad group ideas." This will expand the column, and you'll have the option to enter your product or service. By asking you to enter your "product or service" they're actually asking you to enter the keyword that you'd like your website to rank for.

Type your <u>root keyword</u> into the search box. Your "root keyword" should be a very general keyword associated with your product or service. So for example, if your product is a *"Graphic Design Video Training Course"* then your root keyword is "Graphic Design."

To use the *Google Keyword Planner Tool* effectively, this is what you need to do:

1. Type your root keyword phrase into the search box.
2. For the "Targeting" options, make sure it's set to <u>All locations</u>, <u>English</u>, <u>Google and search partners.</u>
3. For the "Customize your search" section, click on the "Avg. monthly searches" link and then "<" and enter numbers "20000." (this means less than 20,000 monthly searches.)
4. Click the "Get ideas" button! Look at the image below to make sure this is done correctly.

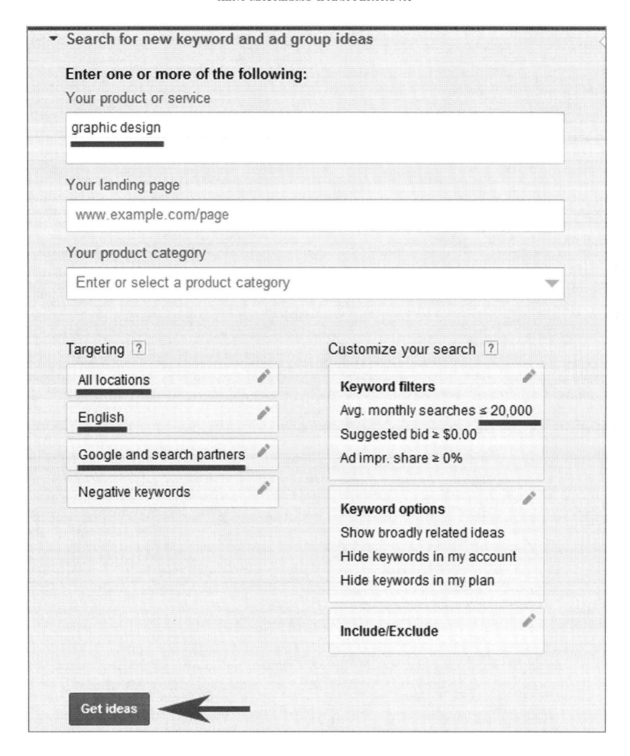

Most people will tell you to only try to rank for keywords that have between 1000-10,000 average monthly searches. I don't agree with that because Google's search results have changed over the years.

Depending on your root keyword phrase, you could trigger YouTube videos, Google Maps, or Google Images to display in the search results.

YouTube videos, Google Maps, and Google Images have less competition and are easier to rank for. So you'll want to hold on to the keywords with over 10,000 average monthly searches for analysis later because you'll find some golden opportunities there.

Okay, so after you click the "Get ideas" button you'll see a list of "Ad group ideas" but we don't want to look at this tab. The information on this tab is used mainly by advertisers that pay for advertisement space on Google. Instead, I want you to click the tab that says "Keyword ideas."

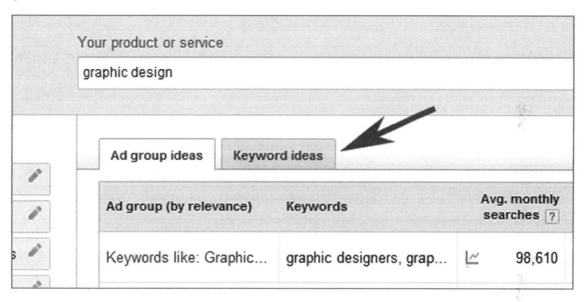

Next click the "Avg. monthly searches" tab to arrange the keywords search volume from highest to lowest.

Keyword (by relevance)		Avg. monthly searches ?	Competition ?	Sugges
graphic designers	⌁	18,100	Medium	
logo designs	⌁	18,100	High	
corporate design	⌁	18,100	Medium	
design a logo	⌁	18,100	High	

Now that we have our keywords arranged, we want to start putting a list together of 20-30 long tail keywords, and buyer keywords.

A long tail keyword phrase has at least 3 words in the phrase i.e. "*graphic design tutorials.*" A buyer keyword phrase would be something like "*graphic design courses*" because that person is most likely looking to **pay** for a graphic design training course.

Make sure that you look at the trends as well. You want to choose keywords that have a stable trend or that are trending upwards. Do not chose keywords that appear to be on a downwards trend. Move your mouse over the squiggly line next to the keyword to view the search trends.

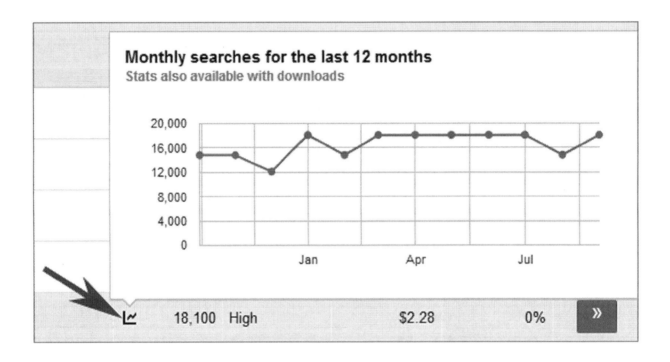

You can sort and save these keywords a few different ways. The easiest way is to download *all* the keywords into an Excel spreadsheet and sort through them in Excel. If you want to download the keywords, just click the download link on the top right. This will enable you to download all 800 keyword ideas.

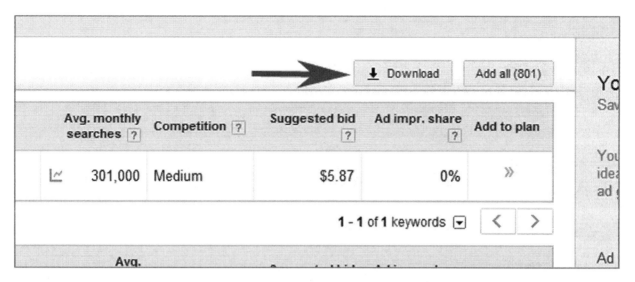

Keep in mind that the keywords with <u>less than 10,000</u> monthly searches will be used to optimize your WordPress website. The keywords with <u>more than 10,000</u> monthly searches will be used to optimize YouTube videos, Google Images, Google Maps, Amazon, Pinterest, etc.

Another keyword tool you can use is "**Keyword Optimizer Pro**." It's currently a free keyword tool that you can download from → <u>http://www.KeywordOptimizerPro.com</u>.

Have you ever noticed how Google gives you suggestions as you're typing what you're looking for? Well Keyword Optimizer Pro <u>extracts</u> all those suggestions for you. Watch the short video on their website to learn how to use the tool. If you look at the image below, you'll notice some really nice *buyer keywords.*

Next, you want to feed these *buying keywords* back into the Google Keyword Planner Tool to check the average monthly search volume. If you combine the power of these two keyword tools, you shouldn't have a problem coming up with a nice list of keywords to optimize for.

Updated Tip: If you want to find even more long tail keywords, you can use "Ubersuggest." You can find the website here: http://ubersuggest.org.

⬆ buy graphic design

- buy graphic design
- buy graphic design portfolios
- buy graphic design online
- buy graphic design portfolio case
- buy graphic design images
- buy graphic designs for t shirts
- buy graphic design art
- buy graphic design posters
- buy graphic design prints
- buy graphic design fonts

Now that we have our Keywords ready to go, I'm going to show you how to analyze these keywords to see how competitive they are.

Chapter 2.

Keyword Analysis

Before we analyze your keywords, I suggest that you install the Alexa Tool Bar. This is going to make the process easier for the next step. To download this toolbar, go to http://www.alexa.com/toolbar.

After the toolbar is installed, the easiest way to analyze your selected keywords is to plug them into Google search. Just make sure that you include the "quotation marks" because we only want to display the results for the *phrase* match.

Your "*buying*" keywords are the most important, so I suggest that you start with those first. So for our example, I'm going to insert the keyword phrase **"graphic design book"** into Google. Anyone searching for this keyword phrase is obviously looking to purchase a book, so it's a perfect keyword.

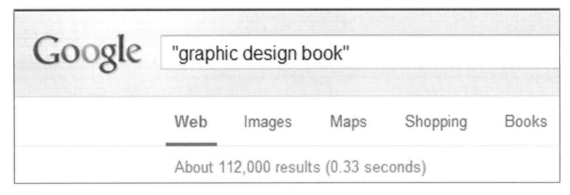

After you hit the search button, simply look down the search results to see what the keyword phrase has triggered. Make sure you only look at the organic search results! The organic search results are sorted by relevance and are based on Google's algorithm.

Usually, the first couple results with the light orange background are paid ads. Also everything on the right column is paid ads as well.

As I take a quick look down the page, I personally believe that **"graphic design book"** is an easy word to rank for. Here's what I notice:

- Amazon has the #1 spot.
- Google Shopping has the 2nd position which is mostly Amazon listings again.

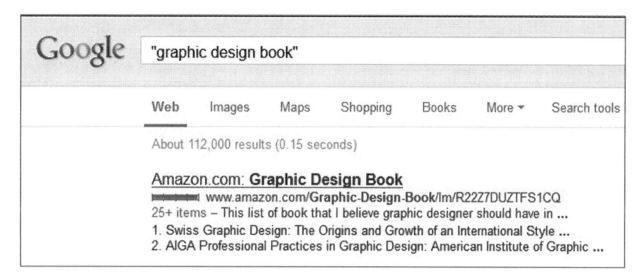

The 3rd and 4th positions are blog posts promoting a Design Book. I can tell these are high authority blogs just by analyzing the Alexa toolbar data.

You'll notice that these websites get a lot of traffic, so it will be hard to outrank them. Just hover your house over the blue tool bar to see the Alexa rank.

Position 5 is yours for the taking! The guy has an Alexa rank of over 13,000,000. Common sense tells me that this isn't an authority website.

Position 6 is a link from Pinterest.com which is similar to Tumblr. After I clicked the link, I noticed that it's just a "Pinterest Board" displaying Graphic Design book covers.

The remaining positions for this keyword are as follows:

- Position 7 is a link from Wikibook.org which isn't even selling a book
- Position 8 is another website with an Alexa rank of over <u>16,000,000</u>
- Position 9 is another blog with some pretty good authority
- Position 10 is an eBay listing
- Position 11** is a YouTube Video

Graphic Design Book - YouTube

www.youtube.com/watch?v=UBkeinCfQVI
Oct 29, 2012 - 5 min - Uploaded by SantaFeUniversity
how to be graphic designer and web designer 2:59. Watch Later
how to be graphic designer and web ...

More videos for **"graphic design book"** »

***The reason there are 11 positions instead of 10 is because the "**Google Shopping Results**" don't really count as a position.*

<u>So to dominate the first page of Google for this phrase, you'll need to:</u>

- Upload your book to Amazon and eBay with an optimized title/description.
- Create a few optimized blog posts.
- Create an optimized board on Pinterest.
- Create a fully optimized Youtube Video.

Now repeat this step for each keyword phrase that you want to rank for. You <u>must analyze your competition first</u> to make sure you're not trying to rank for an almost impossible keyword phrase.

You can also use a keyword analysis tool called "***Market Samurai.***" I personally don't use it because I like to actually look at the search results to see what's there. The Alexa tool usually gives me enough information, but you can use "***Market Samurai***" if you feel like going into "S.E.O. Ninja Mode." (http://www.MarketSamurai.com)

You can also use a free SEO Toolbar available at http://www.seomoz.org/seo-toolbar. I never use this toolbar because I don't like to over analyze my competition. But if you want to really dissect your competition, then I suggest that you use the SEOMOZ toolbar combined with Market Samurai.

I don't want to overwhelm you because after all, this book is called "SEO for **WordPress**." But once you learn how to do SEO for WordPress, you'll realize that the <u>same basic rules apply</u> to Amazon, YouTube, Google Maps, Google Images, Tumblr, Pinterest, etc.

For example, if you type the phrase "how to build a website with wordpress" (using quotations for phrase match), you'll notice that my Amazon book shows up on the first page in position 5.

How To Build A Website With Wordpress...Fast! (Read2Learn ...

▬▬▬▬ www.amazon.com › ... › Management & Leadership › Training
After you buy this book, contact us and let us know how we can make it even better! We respond to all emails. You'll enjoy reading this book. Have a wonderful ...

How To Build a Website With WordPress...Fast! (2nd Edition ...

▬▬▬▬ www.amazon.com › ... › Management & Leadership › Training
After you buy this book, contact us and let us know how we can make it even better! We respond to all emails. You'll enjoy reading this book. Have a wonderful ...

Chapter 3

WordPress Optimization *Dave*

If you've already read our eBook, "How to Build a Website with WordPress...Fast!", then you might be familiar with some of the next steps I'm going to cover.

Log into your WordPress dashboard and navigate down to the "settings" tab. Next, within the settings tab, you want to click on the "permalinks" option.

Select the check box next to the option that says "Post name." This is the best permalink structure to for S.E.O.

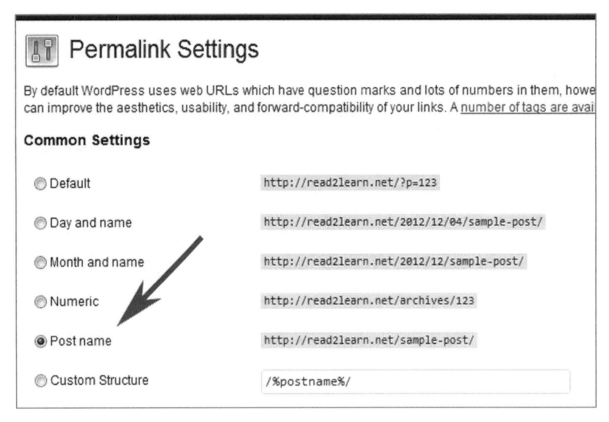

The default permalink structure doesn't give search engines any information about your blog posts. The "Post name" structure will create permalinks that have the same name as your blog posts and/or articles. For example, if I decided to write an article on my website entitled "How to Blog":

- *Default* permalink structure will create a link like this: **read2learn.net/?p=123**
- *Post Name* permalink structure will create a link this: **read2learn.net/how-to-blog**

WordPress Plugins

Here's a list of free plugins that you need to install:

1. **Add Meta Tags**
2. **All in One SEO Pack**
3. **CommentLuv**
4. **Google XML Sitemaps**
5. **Related Posts Thumbnails**
6. **Shareaholic** — have

To install these plugins, navigate down the plugins tab, click *"Add New"*, search for the recommended plugins, click install, then activate!

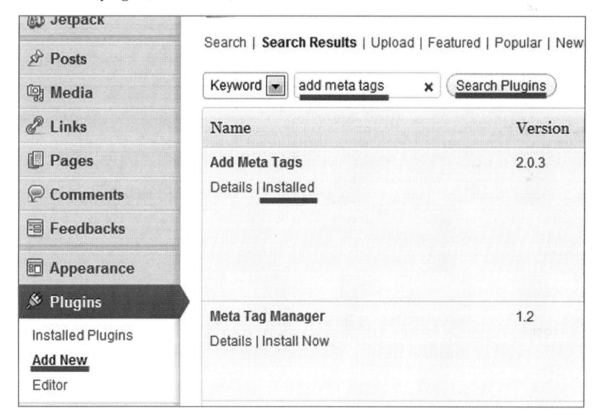

Add Meta Tags

Next navigate back over to the settings tab so we can set up these plugins. Under the settings tab, click the link that says "Metadata" which is the Meta Tags plugin.

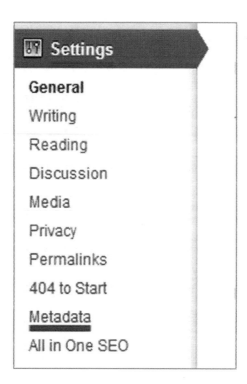

Next, you'll be taken to a page that'll ask you for the following information:

- Front Page Description
- Front Page Keywords
- Global Keywords

For your front page description, make sure that you enter your most important keyword phrase **first!** Search engines give your first keyword phrase more priority than any other keywords within your site description. Next, you'll want to use your keyword at least <u>one more time</u> in the site description.

Front Page Description	Build a Website With WordPress - Want t Website With WordPress Fast!
	Enter a short (150-250 characters long) description **front page**. If this is left empty, then the blog's *Taglir*
Front Page Keywords	build a website with wordpress, wordpre design, how to build a website with wor(
	Enter a comma-delimited list of keywords for your b is left empty, then all of your blog's <u>categories</u> will b(**Example**: keyword1, keyword2, keyword3
Global Keywords	build a website with wordpress, wordpre: design, how to build a website with wor(

For your front page & global keywords, <u>use the same technique</u>! Add your most important keyword phrase first, and then your other keywords after. Keep in mind that spammers have abused the "front page keyword" tag, so it doesn't hold as much weight as it used too. So don't waste a lot of time on the front page keywords.

Leave the "site-wide META tags" option empty. The plugin will handle this feature automatically. Now scroll down and you'll see a few "boxes" that you can click. Click the boxes for the following settings:

- Automatic Basic Metadata
- Automatic Dublin Core Metadata
- Extra SEO Options (see image below.)

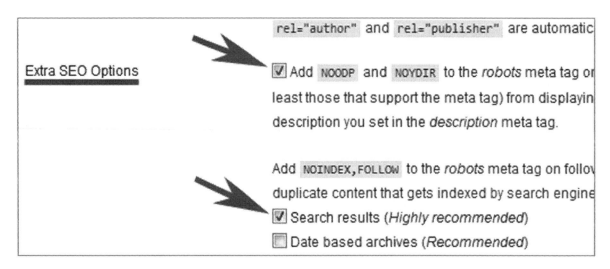

Before you click the "Save changes" button, you'll also have the option to click the box next to the section that says "Donations." By checking that box, the *message from the author* at the top of the screen goes away.

Click "Save Changes." You're done with this plugin.

All in One SEO Pack

This plugin is very similar to the *Meta Tags* plugin. On top left of your Wordpress dashboard, click the *All in One SEO* tab to adjust the general settings. For this plugin, you'll need to enter information for:

- Home Title: Enter your most important keyword phrase.
- Home Description: Enter the same description as the *Add Meta Tags* plugin.
- Home Keywords: Use the same keywords as the *Add Meta Tags* plugin.

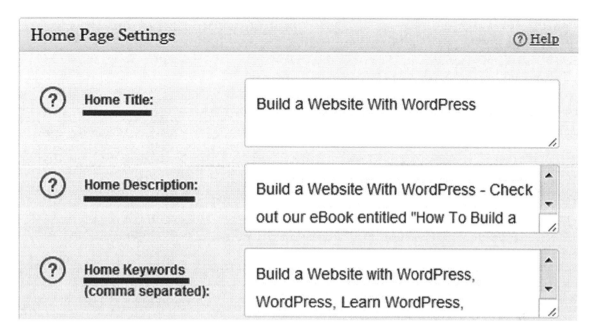

If you scroll down the page, you'll see additional options, but you can leave most of those settings the way they are. There are few updated settings on this plugin that'll make life easier. For example, you'll notice that this plugin has a "Webmaster Verification" area where you can enter your verification code for *Google Webmaster Tools*, *Bing Webmaster Center*, and *Pinterest Site Verification*.

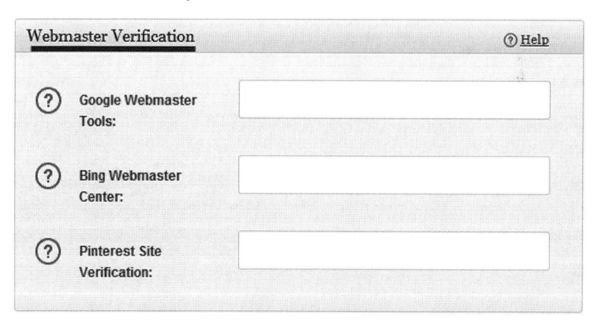

Google Webmaster Tools gives you detailed information about your websites performance. Before "Google Webmaster Tools" can give you information about the requested website, they'll give you a verification code to enter on your website to verify the site. The *All in One*

SEO plugin gives a specific area to enter the verification code instead of searching through your websites HTML code to find the correct spot.

The *All in One SEO* plugin also has an area for you to enter your "Google Plus" profile information, and your Google Analytics ID. Once again, this just makes life easier for you so you don't have to manually enter HTML code on your website.

Scroll all the way down and click "Update Options" to save your *All in One SEO Pack* settings.

Next I want you to go back to the "settings" tab on your WordPress dashboard. Click on the "General" option, and enter your most important keyword phrase in the box that says "*Site Title*" and "*Tagline.*" This should be the <u>same keyword phrase</u> that you used for the All in One SEO plugin.

Scroll down and click "Save Changes."

CommentLuv

Under the settings tab, click the "*CommentLuv*" link and make sure this plugin is enabled. You don't really have to change anything else with this plugin. Just scroll down and click the "Save Settings" button.

When someone leaves a comment on your blog and enters in their websites URL; <u>this plugin will display a backlink</u> to that person's website showing the title to their latest article. That's why it's called "CommentLuv" because you're showing "LUV" to your commentators by promoting their blog articles too.

To use this plugin for SEO, reply to all your commentators from the **article page** and not from your WordPress dashboard. If you reply to comments from your WordPress dashboard, then you won't be able to take advantage of "CommentLuv." But when you reply to comments from the article page, you'll get to use the CommentLuv feature too.

You can actually choose which blog post to display under your comments. You'll have the option to choose from **10 of your most recent blog posts**. That's perfect because you can promote a different article for *each* "Reply" that you leave on your blog. This is good for two reasons:

1. You're linking to other articles within your website. (Deep linking)
2. If people click your links, you'll keep them on your website longer.

If you can get people to stay on your website longer, then Google will rank your website higher. Google wants to provide their users with quality content, and they'll assume your website is good if people click around to read more articles.

Some people prefer to include **multiple** links to other articles within the body text. I don't recommend this for a few reasons:

1. People get annoyed when their reading an article **full of links** that link to other articles. (*Bad user experience.*)
2. You'll **overwhelm** your readers if you link them to a new article before they even finish reading the current one. (*Bad user experience again.*)

3. Most bloggers unwittingly set their links to open in the same window. (*See #2 above*)

If you still want to link to other articles within your body text, you can use a plugin called "Automatic SEO Links." Just don't go overboard and make sure that your links open in a new tab.

Google XML Sitemaps

Under the settings tab, look for the link that says "XML-Sitemap." This will probably be the last item within your settings tab. Click that link to go to your Google XML Sitemap settings.

The only thing you need to do with this plugin is click the link that says something along the lines of "Build sitemap" or "Build my first sitemap."

After your sitemap is built, you should see an image that looks similar to the image below.

Result of the last build process, started on December 3, 2012 7:15 pm.

Your sitemap was last built on **December 3, 2012 7:15 pm**.

Your sitemap (zipped) was last built on **December 3, 2012 7:15 pm**.

Google was **successfully notified** about changes.

Bing was **successfully notified** about changes.

The building process took about **0.38 seconds** to complete and used 4.75 MB of memory.

If you changed something on your server or blog, you should rebuild the sitemap manually.

If you encounter any problems with the build process you can use the debug function to get r

There is a new beta version of this plugin available which supports the new multi-site feature information and download

This plugin will automatically build a sitemap for you. A sitemap will help search engines find all the pages on your website and index them to Google.

Related Posts Thumbnails

This plugin uses the same concept as *CommentLuv*. At the end of your article, the **Related Posts Thumbnails** plugin will display 3 related posts with a small thumbnail from the featured image of the articles.

RELATED POSTS YOU'LL LIKE:

What's a "RSS FEED" and how does it work?

Top 10 Commanding Quotes For 2011

How To Blog For Success

This plugin is designed to keep people on your website and reading more articles. If you set up unique categories and tags for each article, then you'll need to set this plugin to **"random."**

The random settings will display related posts randomly. If you set this plugin to only show related posts based on categories or tags, then this plugin might only show one related post or none depending on how you "tag" and categorize your articles.

Shareaholic

This is a social sharing plugin that allows people to share your website articles on Twitter, Facebook, Tumblr, Pinterest, and other social websites. You don't have to use this specific plugin, but you need to make sure that you have some type of *social sharing* buttons on your website.

<u>Google will notice</u> if your website is being shared through social networks. If people share your website with friends through social networks, then your website will seem important to Google and you'll rank higher.

I personally like Shareaholic because I think it looks cool. After you install this plugin, just make sure that you activate it, and the default setting will work just fine.

Chapter 4

How to Write S.E.O. Optimized Articles and Blog Posts

Writing optimized articles for your website is a lot easier than you think. Some people spend hours trying to pick the best title for their articles, and that's a complete waste of time.

The best titles for your articles are within your **keyword list** that you saved earlier. If 12,000 people per month are searching for the keyword phrase "**buy graphic design art**", then you should use that exact keyword phrase as the <u>title</u> of your article for three reasons:

1. WordPress uses your title as an <u>H1 tag</u>. Search engines look at your H1 tag to determine what your entire article is about.
2. You'll increase your chances of showing up on page #1 of Google when your H1 tag matches a search query.
3. People are also more inclined to click on an article from Google when it's an exact match their search query.

Permalinks

After you write your title, your permalink should automatically populate below the title. You'll notice that your permalink is an exact match to your title. If you click off the title section or delete your title and type a new one, then the permalink might not match your title.

If your permalink doesn't match the title, just click the edit button next to your permalink. Edit the link and make sure it matches your title exactly. (*See image below*.) Search engines scan your permalinks to see what keywords are there. If your permalinks match the title of your article (H1 tag), then you'll get a bump above your competition.

H2 & H3 Tag

The next thing search engines look at is your **H2 tag**. To find the H2 tag option, you have to click the <u>formatting drop down list</u> on your toolbar. After you click the drop down list, you will see something that says "Heading 2" which is the H2 tag.

If you don't see the formatting drop down list, then you need to click the icon that says "<u>Show/Hide Kitchen Sink</u>." For some strange reason, WordPress hides these formatting options by default, and calls it a "Kitchen Sink" which just confuses people.

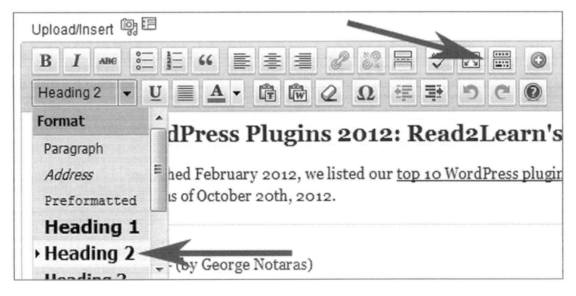

To use the H2 tag correctly:

1. Type the <u>same keyword phrase</u> that you have in your title and permalinks.
2. Select the text by dragging your mouse across the keyword phrase to highlight it.
3. Click the formatting toolbar and select "Heading 2" which is the H2 tag.

You'll notice that the text is now bigger and in bold font. You can also add an extra word or date at the end of the keyword phrase if you like. I sometimes do this so it doesn't look like I repeated the title for no apparent reason.

For example, if my main keyword phrase is, "*buy graphic design art*", I might change my H2 tag to say:

1. **Buy graphic design art** 2014
2. **Buy graphic design art** – Sale
3. **Buy graphic design art** for cheap!

As you can see, the main keyword phrase is still there and you're just expanding on the title. This looks good to search engines and even better to your **readers**.

Do the same thing with the **H3 tag**. Use the H3 tag at least once in your article as a subheading to break up your text. For example, if your keyword is "*buy graphic design art*", you could use a H3 subheading somewhere in your article like this:

Buy Graphic Design Art for Cheap at:

- **Amazon.com/link-to-your-prodcuts**
- **Ebay.com/link-to-your-products**
- **DeviantART.com/link-to-your-prodcuts**

First Paragraph

Your first paragraph should have your keyword phrase at least once! The best way to do this is by asking a question or making a statement. For example:

1. "*Are you looking to **buy graphic design art** for cheap? We've got you covered!*"
2. "***Buy graphic design art** for 50% off during the month of June!*"

Make sure to **Bold** and Underline your keyword phrases. Search engines will acknowledge these phrases as important and give you extra "juice" for these keyword phrases.

It's not that hard to write a sentence that makes sense using your keyword phrase. Just make sure that you don't stuff your keywords into paragraphs if it doesn't make sense.

If your article doesn't make sense, then people will bounce off your page. That basically means that people will click on your link from Google, stay on your page for a couple seconds, and then hit the "back arrow" to go back to Google.

<u>If you have a high "bounce rate" then Google will bounce you off the first page</u>. Google wants to provide their users with relevant and useful information. So if people keep bouncing off your page, then obviously your content isn't relevant to what people are looking for.

Keyword Density

A lot of SEO guys are really big on keyword density. SEO companies have figured out a certain percentage of times that they *think* your keyword phrase should show up within an article..etc etc.

Listen, you're supposed to write for your **READERS** and not for search engines. Don't randomly insert keywords into a paragraph just to meet a keyword density percentage. I personally think that's ridiculous and going overboard.

Just <u>sprinkle</u> your keyword throughout your article and make sure it reads well. You need to impress your readers because they are more important. If your readers like your article, then they'll share it on Facebook and Twitter and Google will notice that. As a reward, Google will move you up ahead of the pack.

If you'd still like to calculate your keyword density, here are some excellent WordPress plugins you can use:

1. "SeoPressor" **$47 limited, $97 Unlimited** (http://seopressor.com)
2. "Blogger High" **FREE** (http://bloggerhigh.com)

You can also search for other alternatives within your WordPress dashboard. Just go to the plugins tab, click "add new", and search for "keyword density" and see if you like any of the available options.

Last Paragraph

The last paragraph is very important. Make sure that you include your keyword phrase at least <u>one more time</u> in the last paragraph. Just make sure that it seems natural so it's not obvious to your readers what you're doing.

Using the same example, "buy graphic design art", I would probably start off my last paragraph like:

"***Buy graphic design art*** *from us today and save 50% off the retail price! If you have a special request, please feel free to contact us using the contact form. You can also contact us using our toll free 800 number. We have over 15 years experience, and all of our clients are happy customers. Order from Amazon or contact us to request a custom order!* "

Lastly, you'll want to add some **anchor text** at the end of the article that points back to the same article. Anchor text is just a hyperlink that contains your keyword phrase. For example:

Buy Graphic Design Art ← That's **anchor text.** (see image below for another example..)

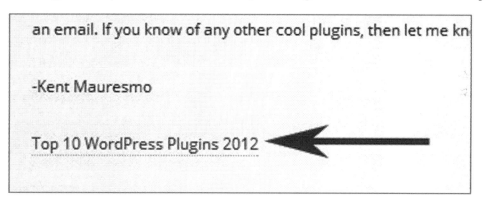

Upload Optimized Images

You need to add images to all your blog post and articles. Images break up the text and make your articles a lot easier to read.

You shouldn't steal pictures from Google Images. Everybody does it, but you shouldn't because you might run into copyright issues.

You can get images **legally** a few different ways:

1. Buy royalty free images. (www.gettyimages.com)
2. Use screenshots (Print screen option www.techsmith.com/snagit.html)
3. Do a Google search for "free royalty free images."
4. Ask users from www.Flickr.com or www.DeviantArt.com if you can use their images in your articles. A lot of people will agree, and they'll just ask for credit for the image.

Before you upload your images to WordPress, you need to rename them with the same title as your article. Save your images to your desktop, right click on the image, and select the "Rename" option.

If you have more than one image, you can still use the same keyword phrase for <u>all</u> your images by adding a number or word at the end. For example:

- <u>Buy graphic design art</u>.
- <u>Buy graphic design art</u> 2014.
- <u>Buy graphic design art</u> now.
- <u>Buy graphic design art</u> discount.

When you upload these images to WordPress, the optimized image name will automatically populate into the "Title" box. Now copy and paste that keyword phrase into the **alternate text** box, **caption** box, and **description** box.

Click the "Update Media" button, and your images are ready to go!

All in One SEO Pack Blog Settings

After you finish uploading your images, scroll down the page and you'll see the *"All in One SEO Pack."* There's a section for a **Title**, **Description**, and **Keywords**. Whatever information you enter into this plugin will be displayed on Search Engines like Google.

Since we already optimized the blog post, you just need to <u>copy</u> the same information from your article into this plugin. So for the *title*, enter in the title of your article. For the *description*, enter your main keyword first, a hyphen, and then enter the first 2 sentences from your article. For the *keywords* section, enter the name of the title again and that's it!

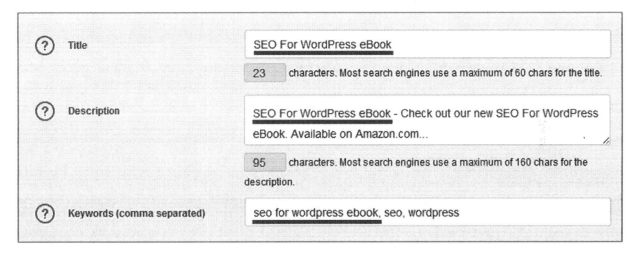

Categories & Tags

On the right column, you'll notice a section that says *categories*. A lot of people ignore this section for some strange reason, but it's very important.

All of your articles are unique and your categories should be unique too. **Your category should be the same exact name as the title of your article**. To add a new category, just click the link that says "+ Add New Category" under the category box.

Below the category section, you'll see a box that says **"Tags."** Enter the same keyword phrase into that section too, and click the *"Add"* button.

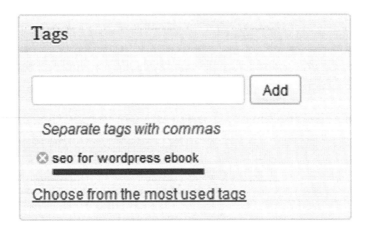

Below the *tag* section, you'll see a *"Featured Image"* section as well. Upload your main image there, and make sure that you use the same image optimization tips that we've discussed earlier. Done!

Tag Cloud Widget

Within your WordPress dashboard, navigate to the "widgets" section. You should see a widget for "tags" or "tag cloud." You should add this widget to your sidebar because it will help search engines determine what your website is about.

When search engines crawl your page, they will see this tag cloud and follow the links to all your articles. This is something that I overlooked in the past, but it turns out that this is great for SEO, so use it!

Tags

2011 2012 amazon blog
Blogging bookmarking websites
books Business Business Guide
business plan clickbank debt Domain
Flipping Ebooks Fastlane facebook
forums Google adwords 2011 google
adwords tips Home how to tweet how to
work twitter I need a business plan
internet success kindle Marketing
Membership Sites mercedes Millionaire
MJ DeMarco Money Motivation myths
Online read read 2 learn
read2learn read to learn SEO

In the next chapter, I'm going to show you how to analyze your own website for free.

Chapter 5

Analyze Your On-Page S.E.O. For Free

Use <u>Traffic Travis</u> to review your on-page SEO. Traffic Travis is free software that you can download from here: **www.read2learn.net/Travis**

You'll have to register your name and email to download the product. Use your real email because they're going to email you a "product key" that you'll need to access the tool.

After you launch the program and enter the product key, the program will start to play a video showing you how to use the software. You can close that video for now and watch it later. That same video will start again everytime to open the software.

After you close the video, you'll be presented with three options:

- Watch Video
- Create New Project
- Let Me Play

Choose the "Let me Play" option, and then click the tab on the top left that says "My Site."

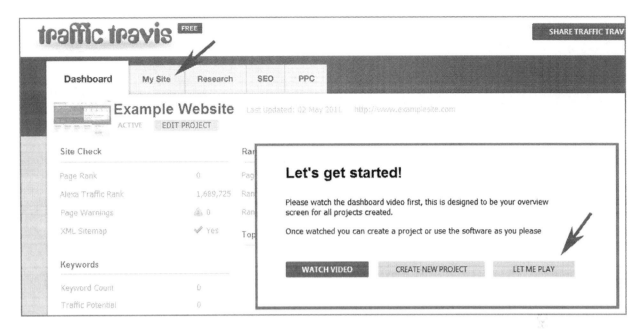

After you click the "My Site" tab, another video will open showing you how to use the "My Site" feature. You can watch that video if you'd like, but I'm about to show you how to use it. On the top left, click the button that says "import pages."

Traffic Travis will ask you import your sitemap file. A site map file will look like this:

- **YourDomainName.com/sitemap.xml**

After you enter your sitemap, scroll down and click the box that says "Import Keywords from Meta Keywords." When you're finish, click the "OK" button.

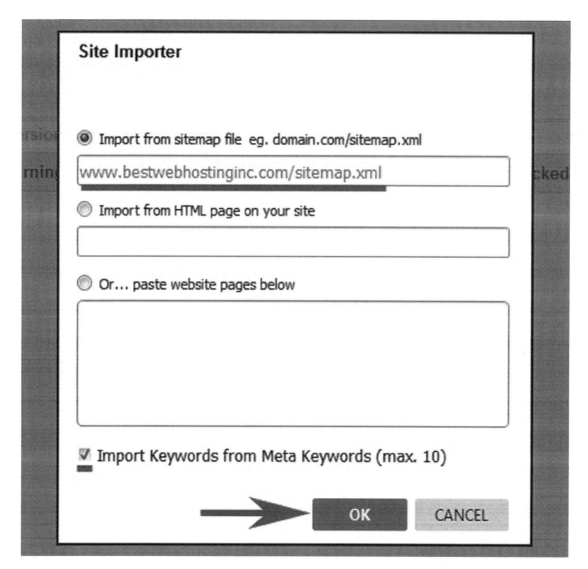

After you click "OK" Traffic Travis will start to analyze your website. After it's finished, you'll see a column that says "Page Warning." Within that *page warning* column you'll see a "number" if you have any on-page SEO problems. Click on the number to find out how you can fix your on-page SEO. Below is an example of an error I found on one of our websites.

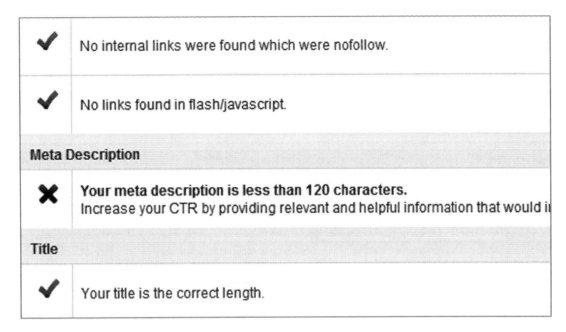

Based on the error message, it looks like my meta description is less than 120 characters. Now that I see what's wrong, I can go back to my website, make the changes myself, and then come back to Traffic Travis and analyze my website again. If I receive a "green check" next to the meta description section, then the problem is solved!

There's no need to pay an S.E.O. company $800.00 to review your website and tell you how to fix it. You can do this by yourself in less than 5 minutes for free. The only thing holding you back from getting on the first page of Google now is **backlinks** to your website.

Once again, you don't need to pay an S.E.O. company $500 - $1000 to get backlinks to your website. You can easily build backlinks yourself, or **outsource it to someone else for cheap**. In the next chapter, I'll go into more detail about backlinks and off-page optimization.

Chapter 6

Off-Page Optimization

After you optimize your homepage and all your blog post/articles, you'll need to create backlinks to your website. A backlink is a link on another website that directs users back to your website. For example, when I wrote an article about "WordPress Plugins", I included a link to *WordPress.org* at the beginning of the article. That counts as a backlink for WordPress.

There are a lot of ways to get backlinks to your site:

- Blog Commenting
- Article Marketing
- Forum Posting
- Social Bookmarking
- User Profiles, etc.

Blog Commenting

When you leave a comment on someone's blog, you have the option to enter your websites URL too. When you enter your websites URL, your "display name" on the comment turns into a clickable hyperlink that points back to your website.

This is my **LEAST favorite way** to get backlinks to your website for a few reasons:

1. You have to <u>read</u> the article first if you plan to leave a valid comment.
2. Most comments are held for <u>moderation</u>, so it's up to the websites owner if your comment will show up or not.
3. The website owner can edit your comment and <u>remove your link</u> if he wants.
4. Posting comments all day takes <u>too much time</u>. Time is your most important asset.

I believe blog commenting is better for branding your website. If you go to www.gravatar.com, you can upload a picture that you want to show up next to all your blog comments.

Igor Donkov · 21 days ago

Simple and true too. I also read your bo

enjoying more freedom. Thank you for

0 ∧ | ∨ · Reply · Share ›

Marta Chłodnicka · 21 days ago

I love this point of view and I love your

trying to live it :)

0 ∧ | ∨ · Reply · Share ›

Some people recommend that you use a picture of your face, but I disagree. I think you should use a picture of your <u>company logo</u> because people will remember your logo faster than your face. So even if a moderator decides to remove your websites link, at least you're still getting your brand out there!

So leaving blog comments is good, but I wouldn't waste a lot of time leaving comments if you're **only** trying to build backlinks. Most reputable bloggers that strongly recommend "blog commenting" as a backlinking strategy <u>never</u> even comment on other peoples blogs. So what's that all about?!

Article Marketing

Article marketing is a really great way to get backlinks to your website. The only downside is that it can really be time consuming to write 100 different articles and post them to 100 different article directories.

The truth is that nobody does this anyway. Most people write an article **once** and pay someone to *spin* it and submit it to multiple article directories. When I say "spin" the article, I simply mean mixing the words around in an article to make it seem as if it's a different article.

Google and Article websites do not like duplicate content. If you submit the <u>same exact article</u> to 100 different article directories, then the directory might not approve your article. If by luck your articles are approved, Google will still remove the articles from their search results to keep their search engine free from duplicate content.

I recommend that you write your article, then go to <u>www.Elance.com</u>, and pay someone like $10-20 to spin your article and submit it to all the article directories. (*See Image Below.*) If you're on a tight budget, then you can go to <u>www.Fiverr.com</u> and pay someone $5 to do the same job.

Richard M.

Writer / <u>Spinner</u> / SEO / Internet Marketing Expert

Philippines | Rate: $7 | Writing & Translation 6 | 14 Jobs | Private | ⭐⭐⭐⭐⭐

SEO has been my identity and brand way back five (5) years ago. The experiences I've accu
span of time defined of what I am today in the field of Search Engine...

Skills: Online Article Writing and Blogging (U.S. Version)

Just be careful with Fiverr because you get what you pay for. A lot of users on Fiverr use automated/spammy techniques that are useless. You might want to give them a <u>sample</u> project first to check out their work. If it looks good, then you can give them your main project to work on.

If you have the extra time, you can <u>spin the articles yourself</u> using free or paid software. For example, you can use:

- http://www.freearticlespinner.com
- http://thebestspinner.com

Whatever you do, don't go overboard when outsourcing article marketing or any other back linking services. If you pay someone to submit 2000 articles so you can get 2000 backlinks within 24 hours, then you're asking for trouble.

2000 backlinks within 24 hours will <u>not look natural</u> to Google and they might penalize you. The way Google can penalize you is by pushing your website to the back of their search results, or just removing your website all together from their search engine.

You're better off paying someone $20 to <u>manually submit</u> your article to 50 article directories rather than paying someone $5 to automatically submit to 2000 directories. My two favorite article directories are:

- www.squidoo.com
- www.hubpages.com

I recommend that you sign up for **Hubpages** and **Squidoo**, and manually submit your articles there yourself. <u>It's</u> good to know how these article directories work and what kind of articles they accept. When you write your articles, use the same S.E.O. strategies that you used on your WordPress website.

Remember to use "*anchor text*" with your main keyword phrase when you post your link on article directories. Most article directories will make this easy for you by asking for your **URL** and then the **Display** text.

If an article directory requires HTML code for anchor text, just <u>use the template below</u> and replace the *URL* with your website, and the text "*Wikipedia*" with your keyword phrase:

<a href="<u>http://en.wikipedia.org/wiki/Main_Page</u>"><u>Wikipedia</u></a>

Forum Posting

This is another of my **least favorite** options to get backlinks to your website. I personally don't like forums because they're usually infested with people passing along poor advice.

When you sign up for forums, you can set up a profile which allows you to add a link that points back to your website. Most forums will also allow you to set up a signature similar to an email signature. When you leave comments on forums, your websites link will show up under your posts. (*See image below.*)

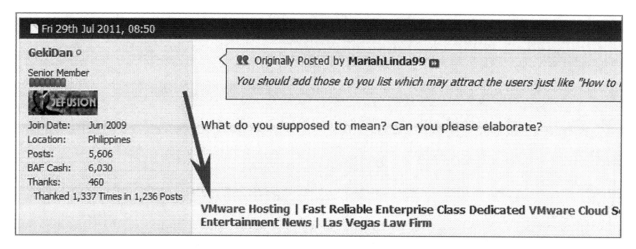

You have to be an active user of the forums to get multiple backlinks pointing back to your website. If you like forums, then this is perfect for you! If not, then <u>outsource</u> this project to someone else.

There are some outsourcers that'll set up multiple forum profiles for you and leave a couple comments on the forums. You can use Elance, Fiverr, or whatever other outsourcing website that you feel comfortable with. Just don't use <u>Freelancer.com</u> because a lot of people have complaints against that company including me.

Social Bookmarking

This is my favorite way to get backlinks! Social Bookmarking websites allow you to share your favorite websites with everybody on the internet. Popular social bookmarking sites include:

- www.stumbleupon.com
- www.digg.com
- www.delicious.com
- www.diigo.com
- www.reddit.com
- www.folkd.com, and a lot more!

Most people outsource social bookmarking, but be careful with that. **You have to use social bookmarking websites correctly or your website could get banned**! If you only bookmark your website, then it's considered "self promotion." Self promotion is the fastest way to get your website banned from social bookmarking communities.

Your social bookmarking accounts should look natural just like your bookmarks within your web browser. Every time you bookmark your articles, you should also bookmark in between 5-10 other websites as well.

You need to sign up for all these sites to see how they work because they all work a little bit different. **This is not a waste of time** for multiple reasons:

1. Social Bookmarking websites have a very high page rank with Google.
2. When you set up your profile, you can include your websites URL for a backlink.
3. You can upload your logo and get people familiar with your brand.
4. You need to know how these websites work if you decide to outsource this task. The only way to know how these websites work is to sign up for them and use them.

It only takes about 10-15 minutes to bookmark your website to about 12 of these social bookmarking websites. That includes bookmarking additional websites to make your accounts look natural.

Each website has a toolbar that you can download to make the bookmarking process faster. I personally recommend using the "AddThis" toolbar which combines all the popular bookmarking sites into one easy to manage toolbar. (*See below.*)

To find this toolbar for the Firefox Mozilla browser:

1. Go to https://addons.mozilla.org
2. Type "addthis" into the search box.
3. Look for the Orange Square with the (+) symbol inside of it, and click the *"Add to Firefox"* button.
4. Restart your browser and set up whichever Social Bookmarking sites that you'd like on the Toolbar.

You can actually watch a video of me using several social bookmarking websites and the "AddThis" toolbar. Just go to www.read2learn.biz and register for free to watch that specific video. It's probably easier to watch the video so you can actually see how I use it.

If you want to take Social Bookmarking to the next level, you should:

- Bookmark any article that you left a blog comment on.
- Bookmark all your articles that you posted to article directories.
- Bookmark every forum page that you left a comment on.
- Bookmark any and every page that displays your websites link!

When you bookmark a page that displays your link, Google will find your link faster and count it as a backlink. Also by bookmarking the page, you're making that page more important in Google's eyes which will also make your link on that page more important.

Profile Accounts

Profile Accounts are created at websites that allow you to upload a photo and a link to your website. This is a great way to get backlinks, and even better for branding!

If a website is considered important to Google, then you want to affiliate yourself with that website. The easiest way to do this is to set up a profile with these websites and upload your logo and your websites address. You can do this yourself, have someone in your office do it, or outsource this task to Elance.com or Fiverr.com.

An example of a profile account that allows you to display your website is Twitter. Search engines will notice this backlink, and people that visit your Twitter profile will see your link and click it if they want to know more about you.

The goal is to create profile accounts at websites that are considered important by Google and that have a lot of authority. I found the easiest way to do this is to go to www.alexa.com, click the "*Top Sites*" tab, and scroll down the list to see which websites will allow you to create profile accounts. (*See image below.*) Obviously you don't want to create a profile account on a porn website, but everything else should be fine.

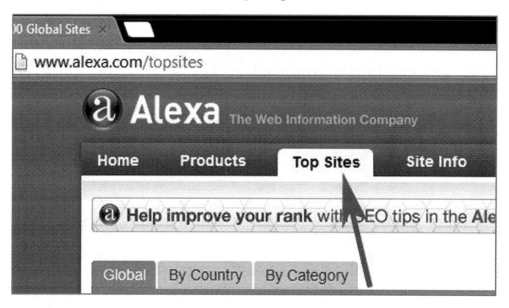

Here's a few websites that you can create profile accounts with:

1. profiles.google.com/me
2. facebook.com/pages/create.php (Facebook Fanpage)
3. amazon.com
4. flickr.com
5. blogger.com
6. pinterest.com
7. tumblr.com
8. wordpress.com (Not to be confused with WordPress.org)
9. linkedin.com
10. digg.com
11. slideshare.net
12. myspace.com
13. stumbleupon.com
14. warriorforum.com
15. deviantart.com
16. youtube.com
17. nytimes.com
18. reddit.com
19. livejournal.com
20. vimeo.com

21. dailymotion.com
22. about.me

Most people don't like to create profile accounts because they're too lazy, but that's their loss and your gain. Some people argue that some of these websites are "No-follow" which basically means that the backlink doesn't count, but I beg to differ.

Google looks at **all** links pointing to your website and it's supposed to be mixed with Do-follow, No-follow, blog comments, links from articles, links from videos, and profile links especially from authority websites.

Like I said earlier, if you have links from multiple authority websites pointing back to your site, then Google will have no choice but to consider you an authority website as well.

On the other hand, if you have a lot of <u>spammy links</u> pointing back to your website, then Google will consider you a spammy website too and penalize you. It's better to have 100 authority backlinks compared to 1,000 spammy backlinks.

That's why I believe you should create these profile accounts yourself to **make sure it's done right**! You should also upload your company logo and actively use these websites once or twice a month.

The websites listed above get the most websites visitors in the world, so I think it's a bad idea to put your websites reputation into someone else's hands by outsourcing this task. You should either <u>do this yourself</u> or have someone in your office handle this assignment.

You'll also notice a lot of *Social Bookmarking* websites in that Alexa list. That's why I recommend that you handle your own social bookmarking too. It would be a shame if you got your website banned because someone from Fiverr spammed these authority websites with your links.

If you still want to outsource this task, then <u>bookmark your website **first**, and then hire someone else to bookmark it as well</u>. For example, when someone else bookmarks your website on *Digg.com* after you've already bookmarked it; the additional bookmark will give your post a "Thumbs Up." A thumbs up is considered a "DIGG" as if to say that they "Digged" your website. That's why it's important to learn how certain things work before you just outsource it.

COSTS MORE THAN IT'S WORTH
Starbucks Introduces $450 Metal Card

usatoday.com

Each specially etched card, loaded with $400, costs $50 to make, which Starbucks says explains the $450 price tag.

4,142 👍 Digg

You should only outsource backlinks to save time, and not because you're clueless and don't know how the process works. If you don't know how the process works, then how will you know if the person you hired knows what they're doing?

After you create these profile accounts, don't forget to use *Social Bookmarking* to bookmark the page that displays your websites link. This will help the search engines index your links faster and your profile pages will start to show up in Google search.

If you type "Kent Mauresmo" into Google, you'll see profile accounts from plenty of authority websites on the first page.

Kent Mauresmo (KentMauresmo) on Pinterest
pinterest.com/**KentMauresmo**/
My name is **Kent Mauresmo**. I love to read, and then share what I learn with other people through my blog. I learn at least 5 new things per day. Kent is using ...

Kent Mauresmo - Los Angeles, CA, USA
www.shelfari.com/**kent-mauresmo**_anastasiya-petrova_read2learn
Aug 24, 2012 – **Kent Mauresmo's** last login was 8 days ago. show recent activity ».
Random books from my shelf. see **Kent Mauresmo's** shelf (16) ...

Kent Mauresmo (read2learn_blog) on Scribd | Scribd
www.scribd.com/read2learn_blog
Scribd is the world's largest social reading and publishing site.

Chapter 7

Boost Your Websites Rankings with RSS Feeds

I hope you know what an RSS Feed is. If not, it's that orange icon you see on most websites. (*See image below.*) Internet users can subscribe to your website via these RSS Feeds, and have your blog posts sent to their eReader device or email. If you don't have an RSS feed installed on your website, you can get one for free at www.feedburner.com.

Once you have an active feed burner account, you can submit your feed URL to feed directories. You can search Google to find websites that accept RSS feeds, but a few good ones are:

1. feedage.com
2. rssmountain.com/rss_directory.php
3. rss-network.com
4. feedcat.net
5. feedyes.com

Just look for a button that says "submit feed" on all of these websites. (*See image below.*) Some feed directories you'll have to register for, and some other directories will allow you to submit your feed anonymously without creating an account.

After you submit your feed, the title of your articles will become clickable anchor text that points back to your website. (*See image below.*) That's why it's very important that you always title your articles correctly because it'll always be used as a clickable link which is anchor text.

read2learn.net
Howismysite data about read2learn.net

Learn WordPress Website Design [Paperback]
Learn WordPress Website Design...Fast! There's now even an easier way to learn design. We noticed that lot of our clients preferred the PDF version of our book bec to print the book out and take notes. Amazon Kindle has a "highlight" feature whic you highlight certain parts of the book and take notes, but ...(image)

Top 10 WordPress Plugins 2012
Top 10 WordPress Plugins 2012: Read2Learn's Top Picks In our eBook published F

Most social bookmarking websites will provide you with an RSS feed too. Just look for the orange RSS icon, or just the words "RSS."

Yahoo Pipes

Yahoo Pipes is a tool that lets you combine multiple feeds into one big feed. I highly recommend that you use yahoo pipes because Yahoo is an authority website. Setting up an RSS feed through Yahoo Pipes can only help you.

You need to have a Yahoo account to use this feature, so make sure you're signed in and then go to http://pipes.yahoo.com/pipes. The next step is to:

1. Click '**Create a Pipe**" on the top of the page.
2. Look on the left column and drag the "**Fetch Feed**" module into the screen on the right.
3. Click the **(+)** symbol on the top left of the module to create multiple boxes and then **enter all your RSS website addresses**.

From the bottom of the module, click the blue circle and drag it to connect to the "pipe output." (*See image below.*) Once its connected, click "Save" on the top right of the page and name your pipe. I recommend that you name your *Yahoo Pipe* using your main keyword phrase instead of something generic like "Kent's Pipe."

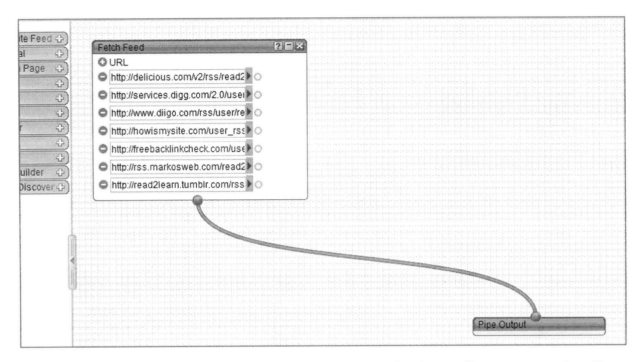

Next click the "*Run Pipe...*" link at the top of the page, and Yahoo will create your pipe. Next you'll be taken to a page that'll show you a list of all your feeds. You will also notice that your Yahoo Pipe has its own <u>web address</u> and a button that says "edit" next to it. You can edit your Yahoo pipe address to add your main keyword phrase.

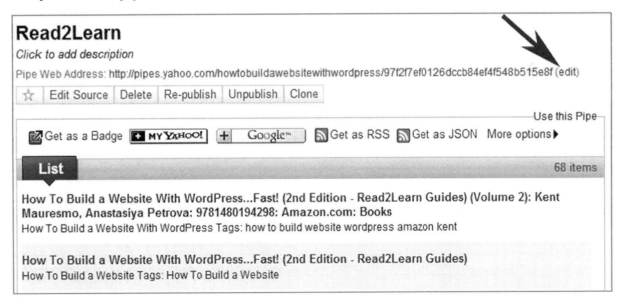

After you change the pipe web address, bookmark this page using all the social bookmarking sites you signed up for.

Bonus Tip: You should also go to <u>www.pingomatic.com</u> and enter your main keyword phrase, your Yahoo Pipes web address, and the RSS feed address for your Yahoo Pipe. Submit this information to help search engines find all your RSS links faster!

Need More RSS Feeds?

If you need more RSS feeds, go to www.howismysite.com. Enter in your websites information, and they will create a profile page for you and give you an RSS feed. You can find the RSS feed button mid-page on the right side.

Now bookmark this page using all the social bookmarking sites, submit the RSS feed to RSS directories, and use Pingomatic to ping the page and the RSS Feed. If you want to take it to the next level, you'll notice something that says "*Other Resources*" at the bottom of the page. (*See Below.*)

OTHER RESOURCES **That Have Info About read2learn.net**

It Is Highly Recommended That You Visit Each Of The Links Below:

1. Aboutdomain.org - read2learn.net
2. Aboutus.org - read2learn.net
3. Alexa.com - read2learn.net
4. Builtwith.com - read2learn.net
5. Cubestat.com - read2learn.net
6. Domaintools - read2learn.net
7. Robtex.com - read2learn.net
8. Siteadvisor.cn - read2learn.net
9. Statbrain.com - read2learn.net
10. W3techs.com - read2learn.net
11. Websitefigures.com - read2learn.net
12. Who.is - read2learn.net
13. Tools4noobs - read2learn.net
14. Whois.ws - read2learn.net
15. Whoisx.co.uk - read2learn.net
16. Whoisya.com - read2learn.net
17. Whorush.com - read2learn.net

When you click those links, they'll create additional profile pages for you with RSS feeds. So once again, you want to social bookmark all those pages, submit the RSS feeds to feed directories, and ping all those pages using pingomatic.

To make the process easier, just copy and paste all your profile pages and RSS feeds into a notepad. Now go to www.bulkping.com or www.pingfarm.com and you can "ping" multiple pages and RSS feeds at the same time.

You can also take all these new RSS feeds and add them to your existing Yahoo Pipe. That might be easier than submitting multiple RSS feeds to multiple sites. I know a lot of this seems tedious, but if you want to make it to the first page of Google, then you have to **step up to the plate** and make it happen.

There are only 10 FREE spots on the first page of Google, and depending on your market, you could be competing with millions of other business owners. Only the business owners that are willing to go above and beyond will make it to the front page of Google and STAY there.

If you don't have the time to complete these tasks, then outsource it to someone else. Keep in mind; **do not** pay a local company $1,000 for "SEO Services." 90% of SEO *companies* will outsource everything I've mentioned in this book to an SEO guy in India for $50.

Chapter 8

Piggyback Your Way To Google's First Page

If you recall in the beginning of the book; Pinterest, Amazon, and YouTube had pages ranking in the Top 10 search results for "**Graphic Design Book**." You can use this same Piggyback method to rank for keywords that are harder to rank for with your blog.

Google likes to mix up their search results with **YouTube** videos, social media websites like **Pinterest**, products from **Amazon**, and images from **Google Images**. So if you want to improve your chances to rank for a keyword, you need to optimize your content and syndicate it to all these popular websites.

For example, to rank your Amazon book on the first page of Google you have to:

1. Type your keyword phrase into Google to make sure there's not another Amazon book ranking for that keyword.
2. Title your book using the exact keyword phrase you're trying to rank for, and include your keyword phrase again in the description section for your book.
3. Once your book goes live; social bookmark your product page, ping it, and set up an article marketing campaign with links pointing back to your product page. Done!

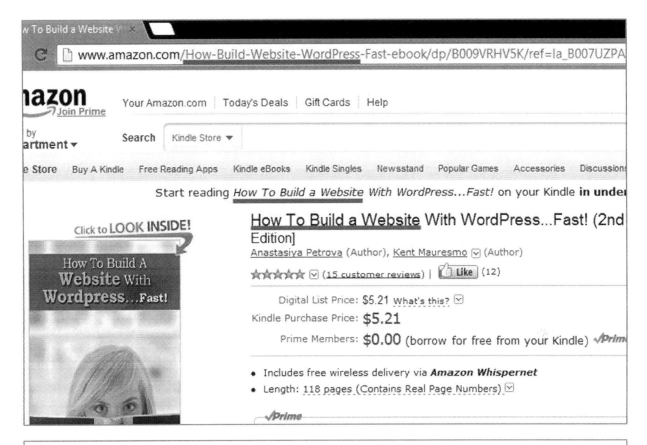

Google loves Amazon, so your book would have probably shown up on page #1 anyways. If you take it to the next level and build backlinks to your product page, then you'll jump to page #1 almost every time.

How To Build A Website With Wordpress...Fast! (Read2Learn ...
www.amazon.com › ... › Management & Leadership › Training
After you buy this book, contact us and let us know how we can make it even better! We respond to all emails. You'll enjoy reading this book. Have a wonderful ...

Take Advantage of Scribd

Scribd is a website that allows you upload and share PDF documents. You can <u>utilize Scribd to build backlinks</u> to your website, build brand awareness, and get to the first page of Google. You can do this easily by:

1. Logging into your WordPress dashboard and click "**edit**" on one of your articles.
2. Copy all your text and pictures and paste it into a MS Word document.
3. At the top of the document, use **anchor text** with your main keyword phrase and enter your URL again below it. (*See image below.*)
4. Click the "Save As" option, and select "**PDF**." When you save your document, don't forget to <u>use your main keyword phrase as the file name</u>. Also save it to your desktop so it's easy to find the document.

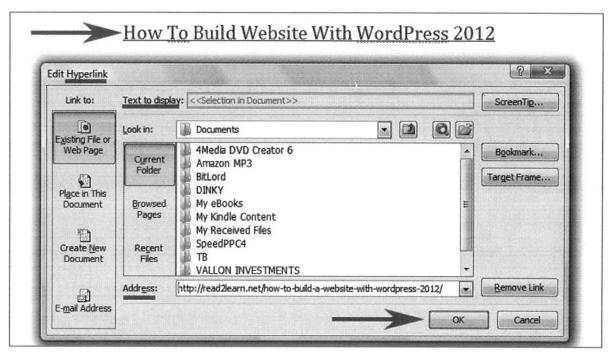

Now all you have to do is log into your Scribd account at www.scribd.com and upload the PDF document. When they prompt you for the title of your article, use your main keyword. When you enter a description, use your main keyword **FIRST** and then enter your description.

If you want the article to rank, then build backlinks to the **Scribd PDF document** using social bookmarking and article directories.

You can repeat this process using other popular websites like:

- slideshare.net
- twitter.com
- facebook.com
- pinterest.com
- google.com/placesforbusiness
- YouTube.com, etc.

YouTube Tips

YouTube is a little tricky. You need to have a lot of "views", "likes" and "comments" on your video for Google to consider your video important and rank it. Not to worry because you can outsource this task to somebody for a couple bucks.

You don't need a master's degree in video editing to upload a simple promo video to YouTube. Just go to www.animoto.com and you can create a professional slide show in about 10 minutes. You can also record a screen cast (record your computer screen) using www.screenr.com or www.techsmith.com/camtasia.html

When you upload your video, just use your main keyword phrase in the title, description and tags. You can also place your websites link in the description too, but make sure that you use "**http://**" in front of your web address so the link will be clickable.

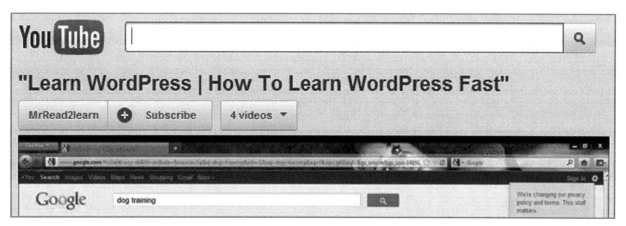

Also, **enter your main keyword phrase FIRST and then enter your websites URL** in the description. (*See image below.*) There are some other tricks in regards to YouTube too, but that's an entire book in itself that we'll probably write later. But if you submit your YouTube videos to social bookmarking sites, you'll increase your chances of your video showing up in the search engines.

Even if your video doesn't get to page #1, creating backlinks on YouTube is still a good

backlinking strategy and you'll get some decent website traffic. YouTube is owned by Google, so you're "keeping it in the family" when you utilize YouTube.

Q&A Websites

Question and Answer websites like **Yahoo Answers** and **Wiki Answers** are great websites for your business. These types of websites are great because:

1. You get to <u>set up a profile account</u> and include your websites address and logo.
2. You can answer a lot of questions which is great for <u>branding your company</u>.
3. Yahoo Answers allows you to include links in the "resource" section when you answer questions. This is a good opportunity to **post links back to your website or your Scribd PDF document** that'll answer a specific question in more detail.

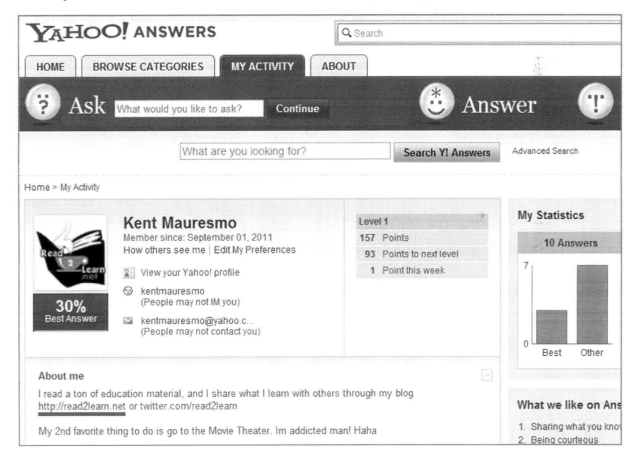

Have you ever typed a question into a search engine and the top results were from Yahoo Answers? That's exactly why you need to sign up for an account with Yahoo Answers and use it for a couple days.

Millions of people visit Yahoo Answers looking for answers to questions. If people keep seeing your company logo pop up and you're leaving quality answers, people will eventually visit your website. If you have a good website with more useful answers, then <u>people will link to your articles</u> and probably click your Facebook "like" button.

There are allegedly hundreds of "secrets", "tricks", and "tactics" to help you jump to the first page of Google. Ironically, **the best way to get to the front page of Google is to help people solve their problems**. When you help people, they'll say good things about you and recommend you to their friends by passing along your websites link.

The more people you help, the more people you'll have sharing your website. That's exactly how websites like **Facebook** became popular. They didn't have an SEO strategy. They just provided a <u>quality service</u> that people liked, and they became popular by word of mouth.

I only bring this up to remind you to always put your <u>customers first</u>. Some people go overboard with SEO and forget that there are people on the other end of these computers. Your articles can be fully optimized from beginning to end, but if your content is poor then:

1. People will bounce off your website.
2. People won't recommend you to their friends.
3. You'll make people mad for wasting their time.
4. Google will remove your article from page #1 because of your bounce rate.
5. You'll have to build backlinks yourself *forever* because no one will naturally link to your website.

So make sure that you have a <u>good balance</u> when it comes to SEO. Always write your articles for the people 1st and search engines 2nd.

Chapter 9

Automated SEO Tools

Throughout this short book, I've showed you how to <u>manually</u> do everything that needs to be done to rank your website on Google. Now that you understand what needs to be done, you're in a much better position to outsource these tasks, or use automation software to free up your time.

Let's be honest; it's <u>very tedious</u> and time consuming to post blog comments, join forums, submit to social bookmarks, submit to article directors, upload PDF documents, and submit your RSS feeds manually across the internet every day.

Below you'll find some excellent automated SEO tools that will do **everything for you** if you're super lazy. If you use automated tools as recommend per the developers, you'll rank very **fast** for competitive keywords.

If you abuse automated tools and try to build 1000 backlinks per day, then you'll just shoot yourself in the foot. The automated tools below are VERY powerful, so there's no need to overdo it.

<u>Top 3 Automated SEO Tools</u>:

- <u>www.read2learn.net/SEnuke</u>
- <u>www.read2learn.net/Magic</u>
- <u>www.read2learn.net/Beast</u>

As an alternative; you'll find a list of the <u>best SEO tools</u> on a single page on our website here: **www.read2learn.net/best-seo-software**

Conclusion

You should now have a better understanding of SEO for WordPress. Every strategy that we've recommended has worked for us and <u>still does</u>. You won't have to worry about Google changing their algorithms with Panda Updates, Penguin, Poodle or Pony because it will not affect you negatively if you follow this guide.

Every time Google has updated their search engines, our blog posts and articles have actually **moved up** in the search engines. The reason for all the Google updates is to remove "Splogs."

A "splog" is a blog which the author uses to promote affiliated websites to increase the search engine rankings of associated sites. Splogs are also used to simply sell links and ads.

So if you're trying to rank a splog on the first page of Google, then you're going to run into a lot of problems every time Google changes things around. But if you operate a legit website that provides a real product or service, then you'll be fine.

You've already have taken the first step by reading this book. The second step is to **put what you've learned into action.** If you still have questions and need additional help, contact us at www.read2learn.net or www.read2learn.biz.

Read2learn.biz is a private video blog. You can watch our "SEO for WordPress" training videos there if you like. It's a lot easier to duplicate what we're doing by watching our videos rather than reading a book.

How to Watch Our Training Videos For FREE

If you want to access our SEO training videos for **free**, then please take 2 minutes to leave us a quick book review on Amazon. Please leave an honest review so we'll know what to change to make the next edition of this book even better.

After you leave your review, send us an email (contact@read2learn.net) and we'll upgrade you so you can watch our paid membership videos for free.

We hope you learned something new, and we look forward to personally working with you in the future. Take care, and I hope you do well with your business.

-*Kent Mauresmo & Anastasiya Petrova*

www.Read2Learn.net

Additional Products by Read2Learn.net

"How To Build a Website With WordPress...Fast! [3rd Edition]"

"WordPress Web Hosting: How to Use cPanel and Your Hosting Control Center"

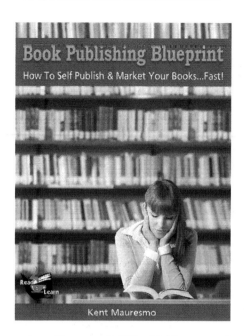

"Book Publishing Blueprint: How to Self Publish & Market Your Books...Fast!"

Made in the USA
Lexington, KY
28 July 2015